Close-Up

Close-Up

by

Quentin Cowdry

First published 2025 by The Hedgehog Poetry Press,

5 Coppack House, Churchill Avenue, Clevedon. BS21 6QW

www.hedgehogpress.co.uk

Copyright © Quentin Cowdry 2025

ISBN: 978-1-916830-47-9

Front cover design by Andrew Latimer

Contents

for Jilly
and the now, not so little
Josh, Georgia, Olivia and Anna

THE WAVE

For many hours we watched the rollers
begin and finish at the coral wall.

It was a vacuous game, trying to spot a winner:
no honest bookie would have given odds.
But lunch had been long and boozy,
replete with talk of dreams,
grand intentions.

From where we lay under the papery
rustle of a palm, the great headwater
stretched out boatless, peopleless
from reef to horizon.

Each minute or so, a breaker would take
its chance. If you looked hard
you could spot the beginning,
a gentle up-swell — from it guess
whether this would be the one
to leap the coral crags,
reach the sapphire calm beyond.

It never happened. Again and again
a wave would play its hand,
rise fast and lustful before
surging headlong to its destruction.

What meagre fun we'd had, faded.
You fell asleep first, me soon after.
An Evian bottle tipped over;
tepid liquid darkened the sand.

Then, a stupendous roar. Jumping up
we saw a huge wave come howling
slantwise at the reef, heedless of the lagoon:
a laughing biker, no helmet, no jacket,
that blasted along the coral crown,
flew a rebel flag of spume.

Of course, its time came too
but, hell, the roar,
that mighty crush of opal.

TOO SOON, THE FLYPAST'S OVER

They don't notice, the kids in the park
   hunched over phones, the couple
not speaking in the café

that man in the donkey jacket
   lurking with his can of Guinness —
don't notice the geese passing:

the way at first they show as dots,
   far off, high up in a thick wet
swirl of sky, then thicken and flock,

grow bellies, wings and skulls
   honed for writing with.
You must tip your head right back

to see them streaming westwards,
   to note how, just below the clouds,
they ink the wind with poems.

Too soon, the flypast's over:
   the birds recede, shrink back to dots;
then, not even that.

None of which disturbs the kids
   taking selfies, makes the couple smile.
But the man in the donkey jacket has gone.

TIE PIN

No longer than a couple of matches
   lying end to end, the box
is of another time, its leather veneer
   thin, blotchy. Folding back the lid

he feels before he sees what rests beneath,
   the creamy pearl poised deathlessly
on a stem of gold. *Hopkins & Hopkins —*
   Jewellers of Dublin reads the stained logo.

A bequest of love it was, a loathsome love
   most would say, which is why it's kept
out of sight, though not secreted, in a drawer
   along with a used cheque book,

some loose receipts, a broken plug.
   Once every few years he takes the token
from its darkened home, places it
   lightly on his desk as an archaeologist

might a curious find and reflects on causes,
   why on summer days it's shadows,
their denseness, their guillotined edges
   that draw. To raise the lid is to free

a swarm of flashbacks: a housemaster's study,
   its volumes of Betjeman, Keats,
of Housman the whole oeuvre, sly
   sweetness of pipe tobacco and an ageing man

gripping a boy tight, his tie pin's pearl
smooth and cold against the pupil's cheek.

THRESHOLD

Standing shoulders back among a bluster
of Dads, it's clear your time has come.
The mould's complete, ripe for shedding.
Mannequin pert in claret top, skinny jeans,
you hear out tales of devil-may-care,
of derring-do, with a tolerant smile.
Earth trembles at your waking Spring.

For seventeen years the breathing clay
has seeped and filled. Arms that were
podgy once have thinned, shaped, found
beauty's line. Thighs have cambered,
breast cups plumped, while eyes that used
to wilt under an adult's gaze, its firm serve,
are steady now, may even risk a bold return.

Soon the final wisps of childhood will go,
soon the final teddy. Before long that habit
of sucking the glass's rim as if you're
still seeking the beaker's ease will just
be a blushful memory. And soon too
you'll know the helplessness of men —
the sunflower's tranced turning to its God.

INHERITANCE

You could, just about, have bought downtown,
found a smart one-bedder close to the sea
where bikinis mix bizarrely
with abayas and onyx-haired children
lick Haagen-Dazs. But that was too easy,
too jarring with something not yet understood,
so instead you moved to a building site
two miles from where the towers on steroids
stand gigantically on the desert floor.

Nosing around your apartment — taupe walls,
kitchen crumbless — of you I find hardly
a trace, save for the fridge's carton
of oat milk, a paper twist of pine nuts.
Fruit and veg boxes remain factory-taped.
Time was that such control, such poisonous
self-denial would madden me with worry
but, these days, a dismal fridge misleads
as daughter and phobia have struck a deal.
Here, in Dubai, you've found a measured peace.

Outside, dumper trucks, drills, are silent:
owners and builders at war again. Yet while
the oil money still flows there's no alarm;
soon the Bangladeshi labourers will return
to add another rib to the nascent suburb,
which, in time, will laud itself as greatest,
home of the mall to end all malls.
For this is how it always is — is how,
beyond the freeway, the city of swank grew tall.

You turn from the window, from the sight
of the Burj Khalifa pinning sky to pavement,
tell me we're eating out. I close the door
to where my books are neatly piled, then step
back briefly to straighten a shirt on a hanger.

THERE'S NOTHING GOOD OR BAD....

why do you always prefer dusk
                    to dawn
                endings
                to beginnings

as it happens the sedge around the lake
                        is lush
and listen let that lorry pass the birch
                    shakes with birdsong

the birds waste their breath

at the start a feast of colour
was spread before you

turquoise turquoise of the Caribbean
                would have been nice
                        good for morale
yours ours

but no you chose   grey
grey of the North Sea
                    in winter

your latest pensée really took the biscuit
the thought we're all just waiting
for a bus marked
                    terminus

even Larkin wasn't as bleak as that

why not throw the dice
try to see the glass half full?

as Hamlet said good bad
it's all a matter of how you think

though philosophy
couldn't save him from Laertes's sword

SEA, SAND AND SELF

Think of a beach and two men strolling.
It could be any beach but this one,
let's say, is wide, well featured —
on one side dunes, on the other, edging
acres of unprinted sand, the print effacing sea.

One man looks intently at where he steps,
observes how wind has chiselled the flats
into a desert-scape of wadi and rise
through which the river,
sensing closeness of gull and wave

gently curls its silted body. Stooped
to get a sharper bead on husks of whelk
and mussel he finds a jewel — a splayed
cockle shell, still hinged, a mermaid's top
lost in a flash of wondrous passion.

Meanwhile, his companion, walking so close
beside it seems the two are almost one,
stares without knowing, unmoved by the ocean
falling in his ear, sees only how the wind
flicks up the sand, drills it into whirling ropes.

NORTH NORFOLK

Strange place, more made of air than earth
   the land is flat, flinty, reed-rimmed, still
   meanly peopled, pinned beneath the giant
dome above. On many days the charm

of neat, stone-splashed cottages
   cast loose in seas of beet and barley
   plays chorus dancer to sky's swank,
its triumphs of light, its endless showmanship.

Beyond The Victoria's stern façade
   bounded by fields mined with birds,
   columns of coated visitors make their own
migration, emerge from Volvo, Saab and Mini

to take the pilgrim path to Holkham Beach.
   There they'll nest on sand and shell and find
   a sort of death. One step off the boardwalk
that leads across a fringe of pine

they're lost, dwarfed by nature's Colosseum,
   cut down to jerky sticks, infinitesimal
   beneath the continent of cloud, beside
the monstrous, ponderously stirring sea.

LA FEMME DE PROVENCE

La femme de Provence kneads the mulish earth
with fingers long as roots. Her smile is full,
indulgent, like the sun that through
the olive's show of leaf still proves its worth.

In her family it was always thus:
the struggle with soil, the fissured land.
Yet now, where once it spat the harrowed vine,
it fruits with breasts, fine limbs, a headless bust.

A DIFFERENT LOGIC

The meltemi has eased today,
tired of vexing tablecloths
in quayside cafes, ruffling
the poise of passing tourists.

In the harbour, a mezze of craft —
some orange hulled, some blue,
some white, all easy on the eye —
cogitate at anchor as old black clad

women would on doorsteps
before the boutiques arrived
and the tour buses jamming
the narrow streets like outsize stools.

Science, no doubt, can explain
why these boats curve so sumptuously,
why from bow or stern
they look like open mussel shells,

their gunwales shell rim fine
but I prefer a different logic,
favour the notion that it's all
a matter of that Cycladic craftsman

who, ages back, had his lover in mind
as he began to work the fragrant pine.

MORNING REFRACTIONS

California it's not, as a matter of fact.

Outside, morning October sun
tiptoes above London's blackened
stacks, its vistas of senile slate
like an apprentice roofer.

Yet, somehow, weirdly
as he discards pyjamas, checks
face in mirror, California it is.
Bath water has guttered to a halt
allowing the mini lake below
to settle, to wobble into stillness.
As it does, strange lovely patterns
form within the liquid warmth,
bracelets of fragile light, radiant,
familial, each to another linked.

Makes him think of Hockney
brush in hand in 60's LA
stoned on colour and freed libido
and that canvas, *Sunbather*,
the pool an abstraction of powder
blue and curling light trails
crowned by a thick line of inflection —
a prone man, naked,
white buttocks sunny side up
to an unreproving sky.

Through the half open window
streams the city's mindless chatter,
a blended clack of commuters,
planes, of snarling white vans
that hunt for parking bays in packs.
He shrugs, then into pristine water
lowers feet, prickling legs, his
hanging cock. The bracelets shatter.

FACES

that fail to sense
       the tread
          of another's eyes

   tell much

      the adulterer's small grimace
   as he administers a kiss
to his wife's forehead

the jowly surrender of
     the drunk asleep on a train
        that man cursing his spaniel

   his ugly air

     and what of your
   chatty neighbour
the road's Mr Conviviality

   its closet neurotic?

for years you've joshed with him
   across the garden wall
       how different he

   looks today

     glimpsed from a bedroom window
   eyes and lips shaping
a frowning face emoji

could we even be sure
   of the Mahatma's mien
      were we able to travel back

     catch him alone
   at breakfast   spidery fingers
probing a bowl of nuts?

MAKING PEACE WITH LANDEG

i.m. Landeg White: 1940-2017

It wasn't the main point of the call,
   more an FYI casually added,
but for days afterwards I fingered it
   as one might a hole in a pocket.

An odd response as the two of us
   had met just once, in Portugal,
where your life, its inter-continental
   meanderings, had finally slowed.

Zambia, Trinidad, Malawi, Sierra Leone,
   your native Britain — they hardly sound
like the staging posts of a dull man;
   yet something close to that pitiless word

was how you seemed to us, a strange brew
   of poets, fled one April week
from a bickering Britain to write
   and take some Algarve sun.

I see a biggish figure in a restaurant —
   trim moustache, colour-shy clothes —
expounding the virtues of Douro wine,
   words issuing from his mouth

like sap from a tapped maple.
   Was this the man who defied a dictator?
Who fooled with insouciance
   an angry militia? Who into the darkened

ticking canefield led the preacher's wife?
  We couldn't see it. Forgetting the poetry,
the scholarship, the brilliant
  rendering of Camoes, we punched low

and mocked our tutor's presumed
  joylessness, the bandana of gloom.
Eight months later, on a call with a friend,
  I learnt that you were dead.

Only then did I start to read your work;
  only then, through lines as sharp as surgery,
discovered the whole man — vital, confessed,
  the vocal heart beneath its screen of bone.

REEK'IN MEAKIN

Walking by the river in a great wind,
willows thrashing like cheerleaders' pompoms,
a face returns across a gulf of forty years.

Meakin, Reek'in Meakin as we called him,
office oddball. The year was '78,
perhaps '79. I was a cub reporter
on the Nottingham Evening Post —
nine editions a day of council wrangles

dressed up as crises, traffic accidents,
smutty trials — he the full grown hack,
though one forever assigned to the swamp
of general news. Dour, fleshy,
he stank like a cat-crapped hedge after rain.

How much did knowledge of that hurt?
Did he wince inside each time he noted
the empty spaces around his desk,
our not-so-subtle cordon sanitaire?
With all that weight, the solitary boozing

his was bound to be an early exit.
Now he's briefly back, immaterial yet clear,
to prod a small but prickly guilt
as gulls, high, black headed, screech and soar.

BIRTHDAY REVIEW

For Peter Pegnall

Yours has always been the right example.
    What about the small matter of the booze
I hear you chortle. *The bottle's python hug?*
    Well, on frailty I'm with the bible:
if all those who lobbed the first stone falsely
    got the Devil's nod the pit of hell
would be pebble dashed with heads.

No, the example I mean is the way
    you've always put poetry first
and a poetry that is fierce and true —
    not an evasion, a kind of reaching out after
lunch on Sunday for Betjeman's "Collected"
    but a refraction of the spinal thing itself.
Right from the start you knew this,

knew you had the gifted seed, had the sense
    and cocky self-belief to tend and fruit it.
Thank Christ you did — the world, don't laugh,
    I'm serious — wheels the better for it.
Better too for that rascally, un-squashable wit,
    without which the demons that have cursed
and cursed may finally have nailed you.

So Peter, on this your 70th, warmest wishes
    but also thanks — thanks by the satin
well fleshed cupfuls, for your mission was never
    only to make poetry. Endowed at birth
with the writer's goody bag, you didn't just
    scoff the sweets yourself: you chose to share.
For that, today, I toast the Poet *and* the Man.

I WILL SHOW YOU FEAR IN
A HANDFUL OF ZOOM CALLS

Irritation, irritation flecked with something worse.
For a moment, seated though she is
on the new home-office chair,
she feels shaky as if sensing
an imminent unravelling.

Why didn't the CEO turn first to her
when it came to questions – she his closest
protector, confidante, his Chief of Staff?

Damn Zoom calls! Before the pandemic
they were like two sides of a sheet
of A4 – she the Brummie girl
with no degree and dinner lady looks
who'd outsmarted, out-scrambled

all the strategists with their MBAs, their smug
talk of May Balls, sub-fusc and High Table.
How dumb of them not to know

what really counts in business —
just getting stuff done.
Execution eats strategy for breakfast
she'd snarl to see off the egos
looking to have a word with Him.

But that was then, before covid shrank
the empire of work to a cataract inducing
chain of video calls. How she loathes them,

her presence now no more than a voice
without body, her face cartoon-like
in a stamp-sized video. When she speaks
it's as if flies beat at a window.
The boss's early morning texts have stopped.

She snaps the laptop shut. It's 7pm on a Friday.
Outside her plush apartment
the sharpness of a fine September day

she's hardly seen is blurring. Before her
yawns two days of time-filling, of park runs,
solitary lattes, of pondering which half friend
might be worth a call. This is her life, her
only life...

MACHINES AND US

In the beginning there were tools
like the flint, sharpened roughly.
These we used to hew and hunt
and hurt. In the primeval forest
we had to invent to survive.
It is hard to say no to the machine.

Bent over clay, the potters of Sumer
were glad to concede when progress
emerged in the shape of a wheel.
The pious will dissent but what more
has lightened our load than the wheel?
It is hard to say no to the machine.

It was hard to say no to the machine
when the factory gate scraped open.
Hungry, poor, we flooded in,
swapped the bone-ache of the farm
for the bone-ache of the mill.
In a sense, we got a little richer.

Before, after, were the machines
of war. From Grecian sling to AK-47,
Roman onager to Challenger Tank —
long centuries of dark creation.
Whether you need to strike or parry
it is hard to say no to the machine.

And what of the present, era of the chip,
of the web, of the high priest of tech
whose works we consume as often as bread
while somewhere, alone in a room, a child
is sick in the head? The pattern is blooded.
Must we always say yes to the machine?

BEDTIME TALE

Shedding clothes used to excite the most.
If passion thickened, hostile feelings crumbled,
would fail to snuff the scaling want as fingers
fought with zips, tore at belts. When mercury
rose, love's thin lipped sceptic abandoned post.

Not now. Tonight, jeans and tops are folded,
shoe-trees found, towels set like waiters' cloths
as if the badger's hour will bring us guests.
Silently I watch you change, get into bed,
thinking of chores undone, the way we scolded.

We are never wholly naked now,
can never talk as once we did. Routine,
the muddying wheels of work have caked us
with layers that hands can simply press, not pierce.
Only our dream selves sleep brow-to-brow.

COLD CASE

Their front door. What was the colour? Blue? Black?

No, on some things they could agree
so it must have been white,
no doubt a beaten white, needing a repaint.

Because, after all this time, it's the truth he wants,

a nailing of fault, he imagines struggling
with clownish overshoes before he enters —
stubborn stickiness of latex gloves.

Inside, there are no surprises: the football

still lies awkwardly in the hall, a pink roller skate
beside, while beyond, the living room
retains that singed air of a stage set,

the climactic scene over, its actors gone.

No-one has straightened the print
above the hearth. From the mess under the sofa
a doll's bare arm stretches clear.

And here's the dining room – sole backwater

in a house which, yes, now he recalls, was always
chaotic, awash with kids, with friends trailing
troubles and he and his wife forever working.

With pressure like that, what chance had they?

Nothing suspicious, no need for charges,
he writes, pressing hard
in his notebook.

The heavy door clunks shut. But conscience

like an odour, slips under it, round it,
restores a woman's face, another woman's face,
and the time after football training

when a seven-year-old boy tells him:
You're not my Dad anymore.

NOT QUITE LAID UP

Grunting, you slipper-creep across the floor
slower than a sailboat in a Force 1 breeze.

I wonder whether in that ancient circuit
board of a head from which so little

intelligible has issued for weeks
the Beaufort Scale still means anything

or whether, if mentioned, you would
as usual get totally muddled,

mistake Force 1, under whose waftings
the sea hardly ripples, for gale Force 10.

Standing close in case of mishap, I watch
you grip the grubby Zimmer frame

tighter, then tack hard to port and slump
into the Stannah Lift that will ease you

past prints and oils of your father's ships
until you reach the downstairs harbour.

There, berthed in your favourite chair
you turn to the window and observe

where clouds head, how the beech tree stirs.
Fine day for a float, you tell your son.

A mild south westerly, no more than a three.
Later, I check the web, find you were right; dead on.

LAST WORD

You don't want to know
how it ended,
the face that was my father's

swivelling around,
a clockwork creature's,
mouth agape, a parched snake-hole.

Dementia undid slowly
at first, disastrously
at the close.

But what should be told is how
amid the raw incongruence
of that summer's day

he supine in his care home bed,
the wires briefly rejoined —
enough for him to say

with a smile as lovely
as a December berry,
Good to see you, son.

And what should be told too
is how, afterwards,
walking, watery-eyed, to the car,

an August sky seemed bluer,
the dahlias by the exit sign
redder, how well I still

recall the young nurse,
her urgent clatter across the gravel,
the small neat hoop of her waist.

THE MOUNTAIN PINES

Finally, all come to this cloud-close place,
place of rock and forest, boundless forest,
where streams run cold and fishless
and wind howls in the cols like a lost husky.

Perhaps now you're having an early encounter,
are here with skis or hiking stick
gazing out over the peaks. See how
thickly we pines inhabit the mountain,

how soldierly we stand. It's as if an army
had set down after years of marching,
though there are no camp fires, no songs
and, even as we speak, the garrison grows.

It must all seem like a Christmas card
magicked to life. But what you take
as embellishment — snow like white
candyfloss in our hair, on our many

tiers of arms — we know as burden.
Come spring, come the melt when the air
fills with the dirge of woods making rain
these boughs won't straighten.

Gall of the old? No — go, enjoy your slalom,
your hike. Just don't be too eager for peace.
We pines know about peace. It's like the sky:
endless, chill and tastes of nothing.

ACKNOWLEDGEMENTS

Acknowledgements are due to the editors of *Poetry Salzburg Review, Ink Sweat & Tears, South, The Cannon's Mouth, The Dawntreader* and *The French Literary Review* for prior publication of the following poems: Inheritance; Cold Case; Sea, Sand & Self; Bedtime Tale; North Norfolk and La Femme de Provence.